CCSS Genre Drama

MW00906714

Essential Question
How do animal characters change familiar stories?

Saving the Green Bird

by Philippa Werry
illustrated by
Rachel Clowes

Scene 1
An Enchanted Visitor

Characters:
EVE, MICHELE, ALLY,
GREEN BIRD/PRINCE, SUN, MOON,
WIND, EAGLE, COOK

Scene: *Inside a large stone mansion.* **ALLY** *is sweeping.* **EVE** *and* **MICHELE** *are dressed up.*

EVE: Don't forget to do the laundry while we're out, little sister.

MICHELE: And do the ironing.

EVE: And make us something good for dinner. We'll be hungry after a day of shopping.

ALLY: Please can I come with you this time?

EVE: Of course not, little sister. There's too much work to do around here.

MICHELE: Don't be so selfish, little sister. If you come, who's going to do all the work while we're gone?

EVE and **MICHELE** *leave.*

ALLY: (*sighing*) I wish I could go shopping, too. All I ever do is work.

GREEN BIRD *flies in the open window.*

ALLY: What a beautiful bird! It's an amazing color!

GREEN BIRD: Hello.

ALLY: (*looking startled*) Did I hear you say something?

GREEN BIRD: Don't be scared. I'm not really a bird. I'm a prince. My name is Luke. I noticed you looking sad, so I decided to visit you.

ALLY: My name is Ally, and I *am* sad. My older sisters make me do all the work while they go out and enjoy themselves.

GREEN BIRD: Your sisters sound really mean. I know I'd be sad and frustrated if I was stuck inside all the time. Can I keep you company while you work?

ALLY: Yes, but don't let my sisters see you.

ALLY *starts sweeping the floor.*

ALLY: Listen, I can hear my sisters coming. You'd better go!

GREEN BIRD: All right, but I'll visit you again as soon as I can.

ALLY: Quick! Don't let them see you!

GREEN BIRD: Here, take this green feather as a symbol of my friendship.

ALLY: Thank you. Now, go!

STOP AND CHECK

Why is Ally sad?

Scene 2
Cruel Hearts

Scene: *Inside the large stone mansion.* **ALLY** *is dusting.* **EVE** *and* **MICHELE** *are flopped on chairs, surrounded by their shopping.*

EVE: I'm worn out. It was so busy in town. Shopping is such hard work, especially when you can't find the right pair of shoes.

MICHELE: Is that why you're so cranky?

EVE: I'm hot and tired. Little sister, get us some cold drinks.

MICHELE: I hope you've finished all your work, little sister.

ALLY: (*bringing cold drinks*) Yes, I've done all the laundry, ironing, and cooking.

EVE: (*whispering to* **MICHELE**) Why is little sister looking so happy?

MICHELE: And look at that feather in her hair. Where did she get that?

EVE: I'll be annoyed if she's having visitors over when she should be working.

MICHELE: Let's hide and see what she does.

EVE: (*yawning*) I'm sooooo tired. I'm going to go to my room and lie down.

MICHELE: Me too.

   EVE *and* **MICHELE** *hide and spy on* **ALLY**.

ALLY: (*hurrying to window*) Green Bird! Green Bird! Where are you?

GREEN BIRD *flies in.* **EVE** *and* **MICHELE** *rush out of their hiding places. They begin to swat at the bird.*

EVE: Shoo! Shoo! Go away!

MICHELE: Get out of here, bird!

ALLY: (*to her sisters*) Stop, stop! What are you doing? You'll hurt him!

GREEN BIRD: (*whispering to* **ALLY**) I live in the Crystal Palace. You can find me there.

GREEN BIRD *flies away.*

ALLY: (*looking out window*) Oh, no, what have you done to the bird? He's gone.

EVE: Who cares? We can't have birds in the house.

ALLY: I've got to go and find him.

EVE: Don't be silly. You can't go anywhere.

MICHELE: There's too much work to do!

ALLY: Well then, you'll have to do it! I'm going to look for the green bird.

STOP AND CHECK

Why do Eve and Michele hide?

Scene 3
Ally to the Rescue

Scene: *The countryside.* **ALLY** *is walking along, carrying her bag.* **SUN** *is nearby, watching.*

ALLY: How will I find the beautiful bird? Who can help me?

SUN: Hello, I'm the Sun. Do you need some help?

ALLY: Yes, please. I'm looking for the Crystal Palace. Do you know where it is?

SUN: Yes, but I can't take you there. I have to cross the sky from sunrise to sunset every day. Perhaps Moon can help you. She'll be arriving soon.

ALLY *sits down to wait for the moon.*

SUN *leaves.* **MOON, WIND,** *and* **EAGLE** *arrive.*

ALLY: Moon, do you know where the Crystal Palace is?

MOON: Yes, but I can't take you. I have to stay up here all night. Perhaps Wind can help.

WIND: Crystal Palace is in the east, but today I have to blow to the west. Perhaps Eagle can help.

ALLY: Eagle, can you help me find the Crystal Palace?

EAGLE: Yes, of course. I know it well. Climb on my back, and we'll leave right away.

ALLY *hops onto* **EAGLE'S** *back.*
EAGLE *flies to the Crystal Palace.*

EAGLE: We're here.

ALLY: Thanks, Eagle!

ALLY: How will I find the beautiful bird in the palace? Perhaps I'll see him if I get a job here.

ALLY *knocks on a door labeled "Kitchen."*
COOK *opens the door.*

ALLY: Hello, I'm looking for a job. Do you need help in the palace kitchen?

COOK: Do you have a good attitude? I need people who can work hard and not complain.

ALLY: I'm used to hard work.

COOK: Can you cook, serve, and clean?

ALLY: Yes, I'm good at all those things.

COOK: Okay, then you're hired. We could use a cheerful face around here.

ALLY: Why are you sad?

COOK: The Prince has turned into a bird. What's worse, he's sick, and no one can cure him.

ALLY: Let me make my special soup. Everyone who eats it feels better.

COOK: (*shrugging*) You can try.

ALLY *makes some soup and takes it upstairs.* **GREEN BIRD** *is lying on a couch looking sick.*

ALLY: Can I come in? I've made some soup.

GREEN BIRD: Your voice sounds familiar. Is it really you, Ally?

ALLY: Yes, it's me. Here, eat this soup. It'll make you feel better.

ALLY *gives* **GREEN BIRD** *some soup.*

GREEN BIRD: (*turns into a prince*) I'm a prince again. Thank you, Ally!

ALLY: You really are a prince!

PRINCE: I am. Stay here and work at the palace. I'll make sure you're always treated well.

ALLY: I'd like that very much, Prince. Thank you!

STOP AND CHECK

What happens after Ally gets a job at the palace?

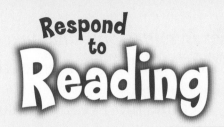

Summarize

Use details from *Saving the Green Bird* to summarize the selection. Your graphic organizer may help you

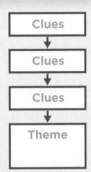

Clues

↓

Clues

↓

Clues

↓

Theme

Text Evidence

1. What text features help you identify this as a drama? GENRE

2. Why does Ally try to protect the bird from her sisters? THEME

3. What does the word *cheerful* mean on page 14? Use context clues to define the word. What antonym for *cheerful* helped you figure out the meaning? SYNONYMS AND ANTONYMS

4. Write about the message the author communicates by having the bird help Ally. WRITE ABOUT READING

Compare Texts
Read a story about an animal who solves a mystery.

The Missing Pie Mystery

Mrs. Marjoram was famous for her pies. Her specialty was blueberry pie. One morning, she got up early and baked some pies for the county fair. She left them cooling by the window.

Soon it was time to go to the fair. She counted the pies.

"Oh, no!" cried Mrs. Marjoram.

The hens began squawking, the piglets began squealing, and the sheep began bleating.

"What's all the commotion?" asked Detective Dog, stretching and yawning.

"One of Mrs. Marjoram's pies has vanished!" said Rooster.

"This is a case for Detective Dog," said Pig.

Detective Dog went to talk to Mrs. Marjoram. Soon he came back into the yard.

"The pie disappeared about ten minutes ago," he said. "I need to know what each of you were doing then."

Illustration: Patrick Girouard

"It wasn't me," said Rooster. "I was busy crowing."

Detective Dog knew that was true because the crowing had woken him up.

"It wasn't me," said Pig. "I was busy rolling in the mud."

"It wasn't me," said Tabby Cat. "I don't like blueberries."

"That's very interesting," said Detective Dog. "Mrs. Marjoram, I know who stole your pie."

"How did you figure it out?" she asked.

"I didn't tell the animals which pie had disappeared, but Tabby Cat knew it was the blueberry pie. That's how I know it was her!"

Make Connections

How does Detective Dog help Mrs. Marjoram?
ESSENTIAL QUESTION

How do animals help people in *Saving the Green Bird* and *The Missing Pie Mystery*? TEXT TO TEXT

Focus on Genre

Dramas Dramas are stories that are written so that they can be acted out for an audience. The text is mostly dialogue, with stage directions that describe the setting and the characters' actions. Dramas usually have scenes instead of chapters.

Read and Find In *Saving the Green Bird*, the stage directions are in italics. They tell the actors where the scene is set and what the characters should be doing. The name of the speaker comes first, and a colon separates the name of the character from the words the character speaks.

Your Turn

Turn to page 6. Find the stage directions that tell each character what to do and say.

Turn to page 15. Write a short scene that shows what Ally's sisters do and say when they hear about her job at the palace. Remember to use the text features of a drama to show who is speaking and what each character does.